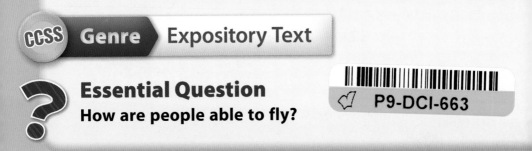

CCSS Genre **Expository Text**

? Essential Question
How are people able to fly?

P9-DCI-663

The Future of Flight

by Anna Harris

Chapter 1
Where to from Here?

planet

spacecraft

People have imagined all kinds of strange spacecraft.

You may have seen movies that show people traveling in flying cars or using spacecraft to explore other planets. These movies could be showing us what air and space travel will be like in the future.

This jetpack uses an engine from a motorcycle.

jetpack

pilot

Imagine the year is 2040. Your jetpack will take you to the store. A jetpack is used like a backpack. Fuel and air are burned in an engine. Then hot air is forced out of the exhaust, or bottom, of the jetpack. This **thrusts** the person wearing the jetpack up into the air.

There are jetpacks that have already been made. One jetpack can stay up in the air for 30 minutes. It has a **range** of 30 miles.

Martin Jetpack

Most experts think that jetpacks would not be good for everyday travel. A group of scientists has started a project called myCopter. The group is studying very small aircraft. The group wants to know if the use of tiny aircraft could be possible in the future.

This picture shows what a myCopter aircraft might look like.

myCopter aircraft

pilot

Gareth Padfield/Flight Stability and Control (University of Liverpool, United Kingdom) www.mycopter.eu

W 30 33 N 03 06 E

080

4   20

steering wheel

seats

The inside of this futuristic aircraft
looks a lot like a normal helicopter.

The group is thinking about how the tiny
aircraft could work. The owners of the aircraft
won't be trained pilots. Experts want to build
aircraft that fly together. Each aircraft could
send out signals to other aircraft nearby. This
will help keep the aircraft from getting too
close to each other. The owner of the aircraft
will choose the main direction. The aircraft will
mostly be controlled by a computer on the
aircraft.

STOP AND CHECK

Describe one kind of aircraft you
learned about in this chapter.

Max Planck Campus Tubingen 2011

Chapter 2

Around the World

scramjet aircraft

NASA built this super-fast aircraft for a project called Hyper-X.

Most passenger jets today fly at 500–600 miles per hour. But scientists are working on aircraft that will fly much faster.

In 2001, NASA built a very fast aircraft. It had a new kind of engine called a **scramjet engine**. The aircraft wasn't controlled by a pilot. The flight path was programmed <u>before</u> the aircraft took off. Its top speed was almost 7,000 miles per hour!

Language Detective	<u>Before</u> is a subordinating conjunction. What is the dependent clause?

Steve Lighthill/NASA/Dryden

A few scramjet aircraft have been built. Some experts think the passenger jets of the future will have scramjet engines.

In 2011, an aircraft company said it had plans to build a new passenger jet. The passenger jet would travel at 3,000 miles per hour! Today the flight from London to Tokyo takes about 12 hours. The new plane would take only two hours.

How High They Fly

Future passenger jet

20 miles high
3,000 mph

Boeing 747

6 miles high
500–600 mph

The new passenger jet will use three different kinds of engines. One kind will be a normal jet engine. The second kind will be a lot like a **rocket engine**. The third kind will be a scramjet engine.

This new aircraft won't pollute the planet as much as other aircraft do. But there is a catch. The plane won't be ready until 2050.

> **In Other Words** a problem. En español, *a catch* quiere decir *una trampa.*

The New Passenger Jet

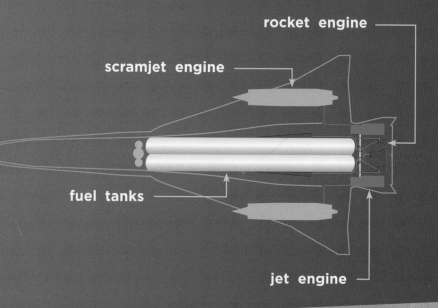

rocket engine

scramjet engine

fuel tanks

jet engine

Traveling Around the World

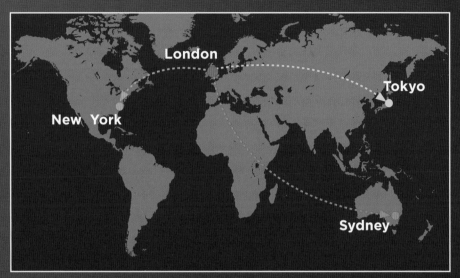

TRAVEL TIMES TODAY

London to New York.. 7 hours

London to Tokyo, Japan...12 hours

London to Sydney, Australia................................... 23 hours

TRAVEL TIMES IN THE FUTURE

London to New York.. 1 hour

London to Tokyo, Japan... 2 hours

London to Sydney, Australia................................... 3.5 hours

STOP AND CHECK

What might passenger jets
be like in the future?

9

Chapter 3

Traveling into Space

In the future, people might take vacations in space!

Today, mostly astronauts travel into space. They are launched into space on rocket ships. Most astronauts go to the International Space Station, or the ISS. The ISS **orbits** Earth.

International Space Station

astronauts

These astronauts are repairing part of the outside of the ISS.

A private company has built its own spaceship. The spaceship has already been on some test flights, but it hasn't traveled into space.

NASA

The spaceship needs help from a plane to get off the ground. <u>When</u> the plane gets to 50,000 feet, the plane will let go of the spaceship. The spaceship's rocket engines will fire up, and the spaceship will fly into space. Later, the spaceship will use its wings to fly back to the ground like a normal plane.

Language Detective	<u>When</u> is a subordinating conjunction. What is the dependent clause?

The plane, *WhiteKnightTwo*, and the spaceship, *SpaceShipTwo*, have been on test flights. The spaceship is the part in the middle.

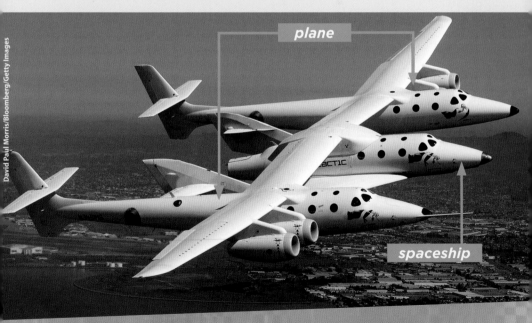

plane

spaceship

David Paul Morris/Bloomberg/Getty Images

passengers

These people are testing out a life-size model of the inside of the spaceship at a science museum.

Each spaceship flight will take two and a half hours. The spaceship will travel 68 miles above Earth. The pull of **gravity** is not very strong when objects are that far away from Earth. Passengers will float around inside the plane for about five minutes.

The flights will be popular. More than 400 people have already <u>signed up for</u> the flights. Tickets cost $200,000.

> **In Other Words** agreed to do. En español, *signed up for* quiere decir *se apuntaron para*.

People have been exploring new places for a long time. People have built machines that have helped them travel faster than before. Some of the ideas in this book might seem impossible. But who knows what will happen in the future!

Could people land on Mars one day?

STOP AND CHECK

Describe the flights the private spaceship will make.

NASA/Pat Rawlings, SAIC

How to Make a Balloon Hovercraft

Follow the steps to build your own toy aircraft.

What You Need:

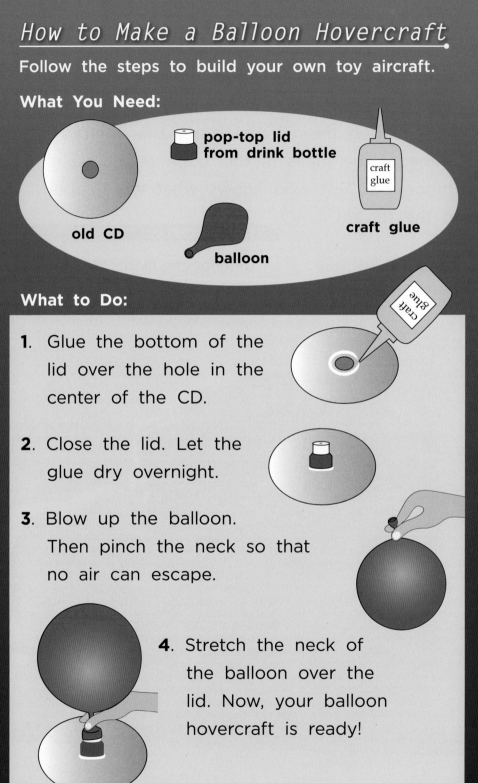

pop-top lid
from drink bottle

craft glue

old CD

balloon

craft glue

What to Do:

1. Glue the bottom of the lid over the hole in the center of the CD.

2. Close the lid. Let the glue dry overnight.

3. Blow up the balloon. Then pinch the neck so that no air can escape.

4. Stretch the neck of the balloon over the lid. Now, your balloon hovercraft is ready!

Summarize

Use details from the text to summarize *The Future of Flight*. Your graphic organizer may help you.

Cause	→	Effect
First	→	
Next	→	
Then	→	
Now	→	

Text Evidence

1. How do you know that *The Future of Flight* is an expository text? GENRE

2. What happens when fuel and air are burned in the jetpack engine? CAUSE AND EFFECT

3. What context clues help you understand the meaning of the word *space* on page 10? MULTIPLE-MEANING WORDS

4. Write about why people build new aircraft. What effects might new kinds of air travel have on the way people live? WRITE ABOUT READING

Compare Texts

Read about how the Norse gods were able to fly.

The
Cloak of Feathers

Once, there was a goddess named Idun. Idun was the goddess of young people. She looked after the magic apples that allowed all the other gods to live forever. One day, Idun was captured by a giant. The giant could look like anything he wanted. He turned into an eagle. He lifted Idun up and carried her away. Then all the other gods and goddesses quickly grew old.

Loki   Freya

Illustration: Luigi Aime

None of the gods and goddesses could fly, but they wanted to rescue Idun. So they asked a woman named Freya for help. Freya had a special cloak made of falcon feathers. The cloak changed its wearer into a bird.

The god Loki borrowed the cloak. Loki turned into a falcon and flew to the land of the giants. Loki found Idun and turned her into a nut. With one quick motion, Loki took the nut and left for home. When Loki turned around, he saw that the giant had again become an eagle. The eagle was chasing him!

eagle

feathers

nut

falcon

Finally, Loki made it back to the city and went inside. The other gods lit fires around the walls of the city. The eagle's wings caught fire as it tried to cross the walls. The eagle gave up and flew to the ocean to put out the flames on its wings.

Idun changed back into a human being. Then Idun gave apples to all the gods and goddesses. Soon, they looked young again.

Idun   Loki

Illustration: Luigi Aime

Make Connections

How is the god Loki able to fly? ESSENTIAL QUESTION

We have aircraft that allow us to fly. Why would people make up stories about using a magic cloak to fly? TEXT TO TEXT

Glossary

gravity the force that pulls smaller objects toward Earth. Gravity stops people from floating off into space. *(page 12)*

orbits moves in a fixed path around an object. The moon orbits Earth. *(page 10)*

range the distance that something can travel *(page 3)*

rocket engine a kind of engine that burns fuel and oxygen to create thrust *(page 8)*

scramjet engine a kind of engine that has no moving parts and is built for very fast speeds *(page 6)*

thrusts pushes at great speed *(page 3)*

Index

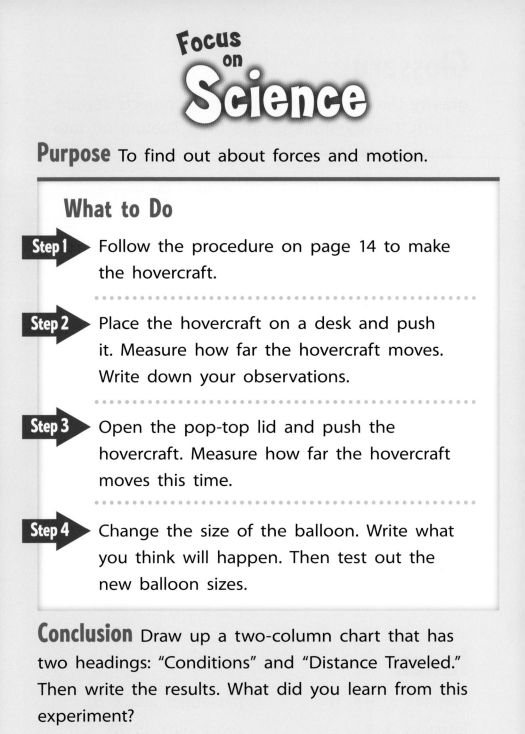

Focus on Science

Purpose To find out about forces and motion.

What to Do

Step 1 Follow the procedure on page 14 to make the hovercraft.

Step 2 Place the hovercraft on a desk and push it. Measure how far the hovercraft moves. Write down your observations.

Step 3 Open the pop-top lid and push the hovercraft. Measure how far the hovercraft moves this time.

Step 4 Change the size of the balloon. Write what you think will happen. Then test out the new balloon sizes.

Conclusion Draw up a two-column chart that has two headings: "Conditions" and "Distance Traveled." Then write the results. What did you learn from this experiment?